Kandinsky

Frank Whitford

Kandinsky

The Colour Library of Art

Hamlyn

London · New York · Sydney · Toronto

Acknowledgments

The paintings in this volume are reproduced by kind permission of the following collections, galleries, and museums to which they belong:

Art Institute of Chicago, Arthur Jerome Eddy Memorial Collection (Plate 21); Max Bill Collection, Zurich (Plate 46); Ernst Bührle Collection, Zurich (Plate 2); Mr & Mrs Nathan Cummings Collection, Chicago (Plates 29, 30, 33); Willard Gidwitz, Chicago (Plate 40); Solomon R. Guggenheim Museum, New York (Plates 23, 28, 33, 38, 43); Madame Nina Kandinsky Collection, Neuilly-sur-Seine (Plates 7, 15, 24, 27, 41, 42, 44, 45, 47); Kaiser-Wilhelm Museum, Krefeld (Plate 20); Professor W. Löffler, Zurich (Plates 18, 48); Galerie Maeght, Paris (Plates 25, 39); Musée d'Art Moderne, Paris (Plate 8); Museum Boymans-van Beuningen, Rotterdam (Plates 26, 32, 36); Phillips Collection, Washington, D.C. (Plate 37); Städtische Galerie im Lenbachhaus, Munich (Plates 1, 3, 4, 5, 6, 9, 10, 12, 13, 14, 16, 17, 19, 22, Figures 2-11); Stedelijk Museum, Collection Marie de Vanstiden, Amsterdam (Plate 11); Mrs. J. L. Wolgin, Philadelphia (Plate 31); Princess Zalstem-Zalessky Collection, New Milford, Conn. (Plate 34); Madame Yvonne Zervos Collection, Paris (Plate 35).

The following photographs were supplied by: Joachim Blauel, Munich (Plates 1, 3, 4, 5, 6, 10, 12, 13, 14, 16, 17, 19, 22); Colorphoto Hans Hinz, Basle (Plate 7); Walter Drayer, Zurich (Plates 2, 18, 24, 25, 27, 42, 46, 48); André Held-Joseph P. Ziolo, Paris (Plate 15); Solomon R. Guggenheim Museum, New York (Plate 40); Raymond Laniepce, Paris (Plates 8, 35, 39, 41, 44, 45, 47); Marlborough Fine Art Limited, London (Plates 31, 34); Robert E. Mates, New York (Plates 23, 28); Sotheby & Co., London (Plates 29, 33); Malcolm Varon, New York (Plate 30). The frontispiece is reproduced by courtesy of Galerie Maeght.

All plates are © by l'A.D.A.G.P., Paris 1967.

First published 1967
Reprinted 1970
Published by Paul Hamlyn Limited,
Drury House • Russell Street • London WC2
© Paul Hamlyn Ltd 1967
Printed in Italy by Officine Grafiche Arnoldo Mondadori, Verona.

Contents

2   Nacht-Gross (literally Large Night) 1903. Woodcut. 11¾ × 5 in. (299 × 127 cm.)

Introduction

Abstract art is the most important contribution made to the history of art during the present century. Kandinsky was the first artist to create a completely abstract picture. That was in 1910. Other painters, notably in Russia, France and Italy were, at about the same time, producing paintings which had no recognisable object. But Kandinsky, working alone, consistently and logically developed towards the creation of what he called 'non-objective' painting. Further, he evolved a firm theoretical basis for the new painting, which reveals him as the major theorist of his time and which continues to have relevance and influence today.

To discover how and why Kandinsky developed towards abstract art is a complex and difficult task. As a personality he remains fascinating but enigmatic. His writings offer few clues. He made few friends and even they knew little of his most private thoughts and feelings. In manners and habits he seemed deliberately to cultivate aloofness and reserve and so far as any picture of him does emerge, it represents merely the tip of the iceberg. Part scientist, part mystic, he was dogmatic, sincere, demanding, and refused to recognise the possibility of compromise. Part Asian, part European, he could on occasion be cold, inscrutable and mysterious; yet his passionate concern for painting, an acute sense of the ridiculous, and a genuine warmth of temperament radiated from him.

He looked more scientist or diplomat than artist. He dressed immaculately, assiduously observing social convention. Kandinsky had a voracious appetite for knowledge and with it the ability to take a broad view of experience, so that what he knew of widely divergent subjects could ultimately be seen as a whole. But his knowledge was not always adequately assimilated: his ideas often appear ill-considered and eccentric, his arguments intuitive and illogical; others, however, shine with the authority of revealed truth and he would pronounce with the authority of a high priest. This authoritative approach earned him the nickname of *Herrgott* among his students at the Bauhaus.

His circumstances were unusual in that he came to painting late, at the age of thirty, after devoting himself to subjects which have no apparent connection with art at all. Unlike Gauguin, who gave up a successful career on the stock exchange to become a full-time painter, Kandinsky had not been a dedicated or talented amateur artist before deciding on his career. He was a Russian who, when he was thirty, went abroad and with the exception of a few years during the Revolution and after, stayed there for the rest of his life. He went first to Germany where he lived until 1933 and acquired German nationality, but then with the advent of the Nazis, as a Russian, an artist and an intellectual, he was suspect. After over thirty-five years he uprooted himself yet again and settled in Paris. In consequence he was deprived of German nationality, but was able quite soon to become a French citizen. Kandinsky remained, however, thoroughly Russian in outlook, temperament and ideas. This enduring Russianness endowed him with qualities which proved crucial in enabling him to envisage and carry out his own revolution. He was able to study the European habit of mind which sustained the traditional western approach to painting. His own cultural background, distant from the one against which he thrust himself, gave him the courage to be radical.

In view of the importance of abstract art in this century, this study will concern itself mainly with Kandinsky's life and work up to the moment when he broke through to what he called 'non-objective' painting. His theories, important in themselves and also as an aid to an understanding of his work, will be discussed and some reasons for the nature of his development will be suggested. Comments on individual paintings will, with rare exceptions, be restricted to the notes on the plates.

Kandinsky was born in Moscow in December 1866, into

3 Umschlagholzschnitt zum *Poésies sans Paroles* (woodcut for jacket of *Poems without Words*) 1904. 9 × 6 in. (23 × 16 cm.)

the Russia of a century ago which was as different from the Russia of today as it was possible to be. The puzzling personality of the Tsar Alexander II, with its uneven mixture of liberalism and reaction, was reflected over the sprawling continent. The Tsar abolished serfdom in 1861 and had begun half-heartedly to revise the political structure of the nation. Cultural progress was beginning to be made in the big cities where, in music and literature at least, something like a renaissance was taking place. Tolstoy's *War and Peace* was being published in instalments between 1864 and 1869 and Pushkin, Lermontov and Gogol were the favourite reading of the educated. Composers like Borodin and Mussorgsky were reaching their artistic maturity. Western influences had been absorbed and transcended, so that in these two fields a unique Russianness was beginning to manifest itself.

The same cannot be said for the visual arts which were at a very low ebb. It was not until later, with the emergence of interesting figures like Bakst and Vrubel, that painting acquired fresh impetus.

Kandinsky's family was comparatively well-to-do. The artist's father was a successful tea trader. Kandinsky moved with the family to Odessa where he completed his course at school and then returned to Moscow to the university. He had chosen to study law and national economics and was so good at law that in 1893 he was appointed a lecturer in jurisprudence. Three years later he was offered a professorship at the University of Dorpat. But he was ill at ease and had no desire to settle down to law. Since 1893 he had paid little attention to teaching, preferring to work in a printing shop which produced coloured art reproductions. He refused the professorship and went with his young wife, whom he had married in 1892, to Munich and art school, leaving behind him as he put it 'all uncongenial and compulsory toil'.

Why did a man of thirty, already eminent in his profession, choose to become an artist and, further, decide to study art in Germany, far from his own country? Despite the atmosphere of cultural revival in Moscow, Germany represented a degree of attainment in the arts to which Russia could not aspire. Although nineteenth century German painting had become obscured by the dramatic achievements of the French, some of the cities of Germany were among the most advanced cultural centres in Europe at the time and students went there from London, Rome and even from Chicago.

Against the general European background of nineteenth century painting, we can now see that in painting and sculpture, Munich could hardly be described as adventurous. Impressionism had made almost no impact, Realism seemed like advanced art to many and Lenbach's 'old master' style was universally accepted. But to a Russian in Moscow, Munich must have seemed one of the fountain-heads of art; indeed to be fair, there were some aspects of cultural life in the Bavarian capital which were exciting and imaginative. Some of the exhibitions staged in the Glaspalast, the Munich equivalent of the Crystal Palace in London, were very advanced: Edvard Munch was shown there as early as 1893. In literature and music there was much promise. Schwabing, the artists' quarter to which Kandinsky moved in 1896, was alive with major talent and genius: the authors Rilke, Wedekind and Thomas Mann were there.

Kandinsky could already speak German. One of his grandmothers was a Balt and they invariably spoke German together. The fairy stories which she told him exercised a powerful hold over his imagination and his first sight of Munich was touched with their magic.

Although Kandinsky had never been very active as an amateur painter, he certainly possessed artistic qualities to an unusual degree and it is remarkable that they did not manifest themselves earlier. He had, however, taken private drawing instruction at school, although the drawings that remain from the pre-Munich period show little more than an ability to reproduce tolerably well what he saw. Far more important are certain events and experiences in Munich which later helped to form his attitude to painting.

All we know about them is what the artist himself records later in his autobiography and elsewhere. He was concerned to explain his artistic beginnings and some aspects of his development in terms of the experiences of his early life. It is clear that in doing so he has over-emphasised and even over-dramatised some of these experiences, leaving us with a somewhat biased account.

If there is a central theme in his autobiography it is that of colour. It begins with his first and very early experience of colour and continues partly as a narration of all the 'colour events' in his life. These have the quality of epiphanies, of truth revealing the spiritual core beneath merely superficial physical existence: 'The first colours which made a strong impression on me were light juicy green, white, crimson red, black, and yellow ochre. These memories go back to the third year of my life. I saw these colours on various objects which are not as clear in my mind today as the colours themselves'. There was the decided 'emotion that I experienced on first seeing the fresh paint come out of the tube... the impression of colours strewn over the palette: of colours—alive, waiting, as yet unseen and hidden in their little tubes...'. And as he took his colours from the palette: 'the brush with unbending will tore pieces from this living colour creation, bringing forth musical notes as it tore away the pieces'. There was the memory of the Moscow sunset, of a white toy horse flecked with yellow, of a trip to Venice as a child where a gondola ride is remembered as a long black shape against an ink-blue sea.

An encounter with folk art has proved crucial to several great modern Russian artists and so it was with Kandinsky.

As a student Kandinsky joined an ethnological expedition to the north west province of Vologda where, travelling by boat, train, river steamer and horse and cart, he had the impression of being on another planet. As a city intellectual he might well have been. The landscape was different from anything he had seen before and the peasants habitually wore their traditional costumes. Kandinsky was most of all interested in the brightly coloured decorations which covered everything, houses, furniture, ploughs—even the lavatories. They were such a riot of colour and design that the objects they decorated seemed to disappear beneath them. Without exaggeration this could be described as Kandinsky's first contact with abstract art: he had the impression of actually walking around inside a picture.

Although Kandinsky later became aware that these events were crucial to his disposition as an artist, his contact with art itself—with two exceptions—was less significant. He knew Russian art well and even copied some of it, but nothing, apart from holy icons, left any lasting impression on him. The exceptions were a brief contact with Monet shortly before he left for Munich, and seeing some paintings by Rembrandt. Monet's work shook him to the core of his sensibility. The picture in question was one of the *Haystacks*. At first he was unable to discern any subject matter, although the form and colours affected him deeply. 'I thought that the painter had no right to paint so unclearly', he wrote, but after reflection there was born deep inside him 'the first faint doubt as to the importance of an "object" as the necessary element in painting'.

When Kandinsky arrived in Munich he was strongly reminded of his grandmother's fairy tales. The atmosphere was, and still is, decidedly Romantic. The twin towers of the *Marienkirche* look down on a city from which, on a clear day, the Alps can be seen. To the ex-lecturer in law the sky-blue street cars seemed to roll through the city like characters from legends and the yellow post-boxes chirped at him from the walls like canaries.

Kandinsky enrolled as a student in the private school of the painter, Anton Azbé, an uninspiring artist and teacher long since forgotten. The teaching was wholly inadequate and in 1900 he took his work to show Franz Stuck, who was one of the most eminent German painters if not one of the most advanced—he painted in the allegorical style of Arnold Böcklin. Stuck was, however, a good teacher and Kandinsky began to improve. One of the last things he did there, the formal portrait of Maria Kruschov, shows how quickly the Russian had not only learned his craft, but had also assimilated the basic ideas of European Realist painting.

After the turn of the century Kandinsky began to develop more quickly, painting imaginative as well as naturalistic pictures. Some of his work was influenced by the German version of Art Nouveau—*Jugendstil*—which took its name from a magazine about art. It was *Jugendstil* which caused a major stir throughout Munich shortly before 1900, and the Bavarian capital rapidly established itself as the German centre of the movement. *Jugendstil*, which had its beginnings in England, was primarily a style of decoration and was concerned first and foremost with its application to architecture, to planning and design in the broad sense. Eventually it influenced painting and sculpture too.

Jugendstil was in marked contrast to anything that had been done before in the unadventurous atmosphere of the Munich of that time. Very simply, *Jugendstil* was designed to create a new attitude, not only to art but also to life. It was closely connected with Symbolism, embodying the belief that art could affect personality in a positive way and that good art could, almost by itself, create or at least help to create a better society. Its forms were based on what its practitioners believed were the universal laws of nature and were thus derived from plant forms and other material which reflects natural rhythms and forces. It was further informed by a belief that lines and colours had an expressive power in their own right and could communicate without relying on subject matter in the traditional sense. It already represented therefore considerable progress towards the idea of abstraction.

One of the most important practitioners of *Jugendstil* in Munich was the architect, August Endell, who had designed the dramatic abstract façade for the Atelier Elvira in 1896. He claimed that 'forms and colours bring about in us a definite emotion'. Proclamations by him and other *Jugendstil* artists show that, theoretically at least, they were abstract artists. Endell recognised that he was in at 'the beginning of the development of a completely new art, an art comprising forms which mean nothing, represent nothing and are reminiscent of nothing, but which assault our souls deeply and powerfully in a way which previously only the tones of music were able to do'. Moreover Schmidt-Hals, another *Jugendstil* artist, actually produced a series of compositions based on whirlpools and other natural forces in which no recognisable object is discernible.

The rise of the movement meant that very quickly the advanced painters, sculptors and designers found themselves moving towards a common goal: the creation of an art which would transcend naturalism. The art world of Munich, previously somewhat sluggish, found itself with an avant-garde. Gabriele Münter, later to become Kandinsky's mistress, wrote: 'As I came to Munich in 1901 it was in a period of great artistic renewal. *Jugendstil* began in its way to attack the old naturalism and to cultivate the qualities of pure line'.

Art Nouveau proved in the end to have been a movement incapable of further development in its own terms, but it left an enormous legacy of ideas from which artists continue to profit. At the time it certainly appealed to the mystical side of Kandinsky. The strong anti-materialist strain and belief in the life-enhancing qualities of art confirmed him in his own views and the theories had a powerful influence on his own. The revealing thing is that he did not completely surrender his own painting to *Jugendstil*, but allowed it to touch him lightly, mainly in his graphic work. This is shown very clearly in his *Phalanx* poster of 1901. The hard flowing contours, the flat areas of colour and the irregular lettering are all *Jugendstil* devices. So too is the pseudo-historical subject matter. The use of part historical, part fantastic subject matter in other work by Kandinsky of the same period derives from the same source.

His tempera studies of knights, archers, birch woods, rising moons and Russian princesses, can as well be attributed to the country of his birth as to *Jugendstil*. The romantic, almost oriental, almost medieval quality of the subjects seems to have served as an outlet for homesickness: 'At that time I tried by line and by distribution of mottled points of colour to express the musical spirit of Russia'.

That *Jugendstil* did not exercise a strong hold over the developing artist can be seen from his studies of nature which he made at the same time. These small landscapes painted in and around Munich are characterised by sombre but luminous colours, thickly applied. The actual strokes of his paint, applied with a palette knife, both emphasise the structure of the subject and unify the surface of the picture. These strokes and the occasional use of a colour for its own sake, felt rather than seen, betray something of the emotions of the painter. They owe something to the Impressionists but more to some of the provincial German Romantic landscape painters of the time.

Kandinsky soon began to feel more independent as an artist and when he left Stuck's academy he helped to found an artists' club called *Phalanx*. The poster discussed above was executed for the first exhibition of the club. It was formed in 1901 to give the young artists of Munich somewhere to exhibit. In spite of the crusading modernism of *Jugendstil* they still met with strong opposition from more official circles.

In addition to mounting a great many exhibitions, *Phalanx* opened a school in 1902 which was run by Kandinsky. Among his students was Gabriele Münter and they immediately took a liking to one another. Kandinsky and his first wife had fallen out soon after they moved to Munich and Gabriele became his mistress soon after she joined the school. She developed into an artist of stature, even though she never became as adventurous as Kandinsky.

The school did not last long, but Kandinsky soon made a reputation for himself and for the school. He used to arrange sketching excursions on bicycles for his students and would herd them together for criticism of their work at the end of a session by loud blasts on a police whistle.

The *Phalanx* exhibitions were of even greater importance for it was here that some of the most talented and advanced German and foreign artists showed their work; for example Monet and the Neo-Impressionists had major exhibitions in Munich. Kandinsky's reputation also increased. His experiments with colour, although not yet far advanced, began to be noticed and a review of the second *Phalanx* exhibition describes him as an artist 'who paints purely and entirely for the sake of colour, displays all kinds of colourist fireworks and uses the most varied techniques...'. He was successful enough to be offered membership of the Berlin Secession and was also invited to take part in exhibitions in cities as far apart as Rome and St Petersburg.

Munich had acquired a considerable reputation in the arts, but Paris was pre-eminently the art centre of the world. Kandinsky's international acceptance dates from 1904 when he exhibited eighteen items in the Paris *Salon d'Automne*. Despite this recognition, it is clear, looking back on his pre-1904 work, that Kandinsky had developed very little as an artist. His course as a painter was slow and sometimes laboured. His paintings are, for their time, certainly on the side of modernism, but they are not in any sense radical, nor are they of outstanding quality or originality.

After 1904 the pace became a little keener. A year before his visit to France Kandinsky took Gabriele Münter to Rapallo on the Italian Riviera and then on to Tunisia and the old city of Kairuan. The landscapes from the Rapallo visit, although not very different from earlier ones, do show a greater sureness and freedom of touch and a lighter and less naturalistic approach to colour (plate 5).

This was strengthened after the Paris visit. Kandinsky had been to the French capital twice before—in 1889 and 1892—but these visits seem to have had little effect on him. But in 1904 the Neo-Impressionists he saw there and whom he later invited to show in Munich, clearly convinced him that he needed to purify his colours more radically and to remove them even further from the colours of nature. Although still painting his fairy tale scenes from time to time, his landscapes become now decidedly brighter and more controlled; narrative subject matter begins to disappear gradually from his work. The crucial phase was just over the horizon and it would not be long before Kandinsky would emerge as a mature artist after a long and difficult struggle.

There is evidence that Kandinsky had been ill at ease in Munich, that he was frustrated because his painting was not developing as fast as his thinking and that he felt to a certain extent misled by the experiments of other artists in his circle. He and Münter had known about the village of Murnau, in Upper Bavaria, for some time. It was isolated and picturesque. He could leave behind him the complex art politics of the city, concentrate all his energies on work and follow his own inclinations without interference. In 1908 Kandinsky and Münter therefore decided to buy a house in Murnau and

4   Reiter (Rider) 1907. Woodcut. 5¼ × 5¼ in. (14 × 14 cm.)   5   Mönch (Monk) 1907. Two-colour woodcut. 9½ × 2½ in. (65 × 24 cm.)

6 Mitgliedskarte der Neue Künstlervereinigung München
(membership card for the 'New Artists' Association of Munich')

of him in a riot of brilliance. Colour in these paintings is used almost entirely for emotional reasons and applied in large slabs or chunks which say little or nothing about the form, weight and mass of the objects they decorate. The light is brilliant, almost electrically hard. No longer working with his palette knife, Kandinsky now lays on his colour in a series of directional brush strokes. Again these say less about the objects they describe than about the artist's own emotions (plates 8, 9, 10, 11).

The Murnau landscapes have been called Fauve and their implicit violence and harshness of colour certainly have something in common with the work of, say, Vlaminck. But they are essentially un-French in the directness and primitiveness of their expression. Kandinsky said at this time that 'if the artist has outer and inner eyes for nature, nature rewards him by giving him inspiration', and this in part explains the intentions behind the Murnau landscapes. In these pictures he is interested in a poetic interpretation of nature where the superficial appearance of objects reveals something of the universal spirit of Nature. The tension between the inner and outer worlds has decreased, for the outer forms of the inner spirit now reflect what lies behind them. It was not now such a big step to the evolution of non-realistic forms which would directly communicate an experience of the inner, spiritual world.

The trouble was, and indeed still is, that non-figurative art, relying for its effects on shapes, colours and lines which have no apparent connection with the real world, can so easily degenerate into mere pattern-making, an emasculated object, visually satisfying but spiritually dead. Kandinsky recognised the danger only too well: 'If we begin at once to break the bonds that bind us to nature and to devote ourselves purely to combination of pure colour and independent form, we shall produce works which are mere geometric design, resembling something like a necktie or a carpet.

live there for the greater part of each year. The change in surroundings facilitated the break-through that the artist was seeking.

Compared with earlier paintings the Murnau work is hot, passionate and unrestrained. In the landscapes and village scenes which Kandinsky did here colour is finally liberated from its traditional context, from the confines of naturalism and from the restrictive influence of his own innate reserve. Here he allowed his natural feeling for colour to pour out

Beauty of form and colour is not sufficient aim in itself, despite the assertions of pure aesthetics or even of naturalists obsessed with the idea of "beauty". It is because our painting is still at an elementary stage that we are so little able to be moved by wholly autonomous colour and form composition. The nerve vibrations are there (as we feel when confronted by applied art), but they get no further than the nerves because the corresponding vibrations of the spirit which they call forth are weak. When we remember, however, that spiritual experience is quickening, that positive science, the firmest basis of human thought is tottering, that dissolution of matter is imminent, we have reason to hope that the hour of pure composition is not far away. The first stage has arrived.' Kandinsky *Concerning the Spiritual in Art*.

This in part explains why the final transition to nonobjective art was so slow. Kandinsky continued to paint in the Murnau style and at the same time produced work which was more experimental. The landscapes from Murnau changed too, becoming more completely charged with emotion and so less like the subjects which inspired them. As Kandinsky moved further away from a realistic rendering of what his eyes saw, he began to transform his pictures into evocative objects, from the construction of which an inner sense would be evoked which was intended to touch the spectator in the same way as the pictures of nature itself. Through the raw material, colour, form and line, painting came close to music and Kandinsky hoped that it would eventually be able to express experience as directly as music with its tones, melodic construction and rhythm.

For these experimental pictures Kandinsky ceased to use objective titles and chose instead musical terms: 'improvisation' and 'composition'. His pictures were now meant to have life, not through what they represented but through effects unique to art, through colour vibrations and linear configurations which attempted to make visible a dramatic or lyrical state of the sensibilities. The 'improvisations' were what the name implies: spontaneous expressions of experience. The 'compositions' on the other hand crystallised slowly out of preliminary studies and sketches and in them the conscious mind played a considerable part. Kandinsky also at this time discriminated between two further types of painting, the 'melodic' and the 'symphonic'. In the melodic the composition is based on a single form, in the symphonic on several forms subordinated to an overall design.

It is not difficult to trace the lineage of the abstract forms Kandinsky developed. They come from some of the motifs which appear in his earlier landscapes and narrative paintings. A horse and rider is first translated into a paraphrased image and then into a complex of lines. Trees, hills, groups of people are rendered in the same way, each line having a distinct character and a different source.

Certain features in the early abstract *Compositions* are reminiscent of the music of Wagner which Kandinsky so greatly admired. Just as Wagner's music calls forth associations in the listener's mind, so the tonal play of colour and line in the paintings stimulates associations with the real world—horses, Russian churches, country scenes. But the paintings quickly become more difficult to decipher and the music of Schoenberg rather than of Wagner comes to mind. Schoenberg was a friend of Kandinsky and developed his theories of modern music in close collaboration with him and at the same time as Kandinsky was struggling with his theories of art. Schoenberg's music, like Kandinsky's first truly abstract painting, exists solely for itself in its own terms and does not call forth associations with anything outside itself.

Kandinsky made the transition to abstract painting with the greatest caution. It took him four years—he was painting landscapes as late as 1913. This is not surprising. He was working alone, his ideas were revolutionary and they needed courage and strength of will to put into practice. He was creating literally from the void, treading unexplored paths.

The creation of a non-figurative manner of painting was not an intuitive process. Kandinsky was as much thinker as artist; he thought before he acted and he had worked out the basis of and the terms for the new art, long before he tried to put them into practice. Before discussing his theories in greater detail, some of the experiences which made Kandinsky believe in the necessity of an abstract art must be described and then something of the contemporary climate of ideas which further stimulated his thought.

We have already considered those early Russian experiences—of colour and folk-art—which Kandinsky says in his autobiography helped to mould his thought and shape his attitude to art. Later experiences were equally crucial and the story he tells about returning to the house at Murnau after a sketching expedition, calls to mind his earlier contact with Monet in Moscow. He came back to his studio in the half-light to be confronted with an object of dazzling beauty on his easel. Once again he could make out no subject, once again he was profoundly affected by the shapes and colours in the picture. Suddenly his belief in the ultimate redundancy of the traditional 'subject' of a picture was confirmed. It was only then he realised that the painting was resting on its side.

In Moscow Kandinsky had interests apart from his professional concern with law and his amateur interest in art. He knew a great deal about science and was always in touch with the latest scientific discoveries. When he came to Munich it was a period of great upheaval in the scientific world and a difficult and major change of direction was taking place.

One of the most revolutionary scientific events in the early years of the century was the publication of Max Planck's Quantum Theory. Before Planck, scientists regarded matter as indestructible, the ultimate, irreducible fact of the universe. Planck put forward the theory that matter was rather electri-city in constant motion, that matter was energy and that the universe was in a state of flux. Planck therefore not only called into question the very existence of the real world, but also the authority of science itself. Einstein's general theory of relativity and Freud's discovery of the subconscious had similar effects. The 'reality' of the visible world appeared more and more to consist in the human faculty of apperception and was therefore no longer regarded as objective fact. And if scientists proved to be fallible, and the old and trusted picture of the world could so easily be shattered, then Kandinsky could feel that he had the right to destroy the old 'realistic' type of art and create his own according to the principles of the 'spirit' and the 'soul', principles which, he believed, were much better founded.

When the atom was split Kandinsky was even more determined: 'the destruction of the atom seemed to me to be the same as the destruction of the world... science to me appeared to be dead: its most important basis was only a lunacy, a mistake perpetrated by learned men... who blindly mistook one object for another'.

The metaphysical, anti-materialistic side of Kandinsky's personality, which was strengthened by what he knew of science, was further encouraged by his contact with the theosophist Rudolph Steiner. One of Kandinsky's pupils at the *Phalanx* school was a disciple of Steiner. She introduced her art tutor to Steiner's lectures in Munich and to his writings.

Steiner, like Kandinsky, believed in the impending doom of the world and that the salvation of humanity lay in the rediscovery of the spirit, of the soul of man and the hidden laws of the universe. Steiner even formulated a theosophical theory of art and his attitude to colour, which was conditioned by Goethe's own colour system, helped Kandinsky solve his own problems with colour. Steiner convinced Kandinsky that the artist's task was to raise the world to the sphere of the divine and spiritual, to re-establish its contact with the Great Chain of Being. According to Steiner '...everyone who immerses himself in the hidden internal treasures of his art is an enviable co-worker on the spiritual pyramid which will reach to heaven'.

It was in any case easier for a Russian to conceive of an abstract art than for someone rooted in the European tradition. It may be difficult to believe, but the idea of perspective and illusionistic art in general was quite foreign to the Russian artist. It was adopted rather late, taken consciously as an influence from the West, and was still regarded as something very Western even at the turn of the century. Kandinsky had grown up understanding the world of icons, believing that a painted picture was in the first place a painted object and did not have primarily an imitative function. In Europe artists created facts, in Russia mysteries, and in 1918 in the German version of his autobiography, Kandinsky adds the footnote: 'the long Russian word for creation, *proisvedenie*, so different from its shorter counterparts in English, French and German, express for me the whole history and process of creation, lengthy, mysterious, infinitely complex and fore-shadowed by divine predestination'. He later described art as 'the mysterious expression of the mysterious'.

These ideas helped to form the general philosophical background from which Kandinsky derived the material for his first and most important theoretical statement, *Concerning the Spiritual in Art*. This was written between 1910 and 1911 and was published in 1912. It thus belongs to the same historical moment as Joyce's *Ulysses* and Schoenberg's *Harmonielehre*. Each in its way was as much an expression of the spirit of modernism as the theories of Planck, Einstein and Freud. Schoenberg, who was something of a painter as well as a composer, and Kandinsky worked closely together on their respective manifestos and both attempted to reverse completely traditional thinking in music and art.

7   Komposition II (Composition II) 1911. Woodcut. 5¾ × 8¼ in.

8   Lyrisches II (Lyrical II) 1911. Colour woodcut. 5⅞ × 8½ in

9 Almanac der Blaue Reiter (cover for Almanac of the Blue Rider) 1912. Colour woodcut. 11×8¼ in. (28×21 cm.)

Kandinsky was convinced that traditional representational art was dead and he was equally sure that non-objective art needed a subject in order to survive. The subject had, of course, to be different; it needed to be an experience, an emotion or spiritual disposition which could be communicated through an abstract language. To him, as we have seen, the reality of the 'soul' was an unquestionable fact, and the first part of *Concerning the Spiritual in Art* deals with the spiritual foundation of art and words like 'soul', 'life' and 'spirit' occur constantly throughout the book. The second part deals with the formal conditions of creation: how the 'spirit' could be communicated.

As an anti-materialist Kandinsky believed that gross matter, the outward shape of nature, both concealed and revealed the great spirit of the universe. To communicate demanded as pure a means of expression as possible; the purer, the more direct the means of expression and communication. It was an old idea that the purest of all forms of art was music because it did not rely on anything outside itself for its effects. Poetry relied on words which had a generally agreed meaning. Painting relied on the real world which it represented. But music, free from any exclusive meanings, was pure. It was moreover a system which could be explained mathematically. It is its very purity, the directness of its expression, that Walter Pater was thinking of when he said that 'all art aspires to the condition of music'.

So Kandinsky tried to see painting in musical terms, to isolate the various parts of its language and to see how they could be purified and made to communicate directly. We have seen that he used musical terms as titles for his early abstract experiments. He began then, in his first treatise, with the problems of colour. It had long been thought that there were certain connections between the senses, and that what was heard also has an effect on what was seen and felt. Various writers had even gone so far as to invent tables establishing direct equivalents for lines, colours and music. The composer, Scriabin, had in fact written scores which included directions for a colour accompaniment to his music. Moreover, lines, colours and sounds could have an effect on the emotions. Drooping slack lines, for example, are melancholic and have their colour equivalent in blue and sombre tones. In *Concerning the Spiritual* yellow is defined as an 'intense trumpet blast' of quite earthy expressiveness and by its nature springing forth from the canvas, whereas blue is a celestial organ sound which touches the depths. This single example explains something of Kandinsky's theory.

We have already seen how Steiner and Goethe helped him to come to certain conclusions about colour and the spiritual elements in art. But what he says about the emotional effects of colour also reveals a profound knowledge of colour theory and of Delacroix, Charles Blanc and Seurat. The associative connection between colour and music was also a favourite idea of the German Romantics. Wagner's concept of the *Gesamtkunstwerk*, which Kandinsky clearly knew, is the best known example of this form of aesthetic. In this respect *Concerning the Spiritual in Art* represents a further development of a well established line of thought. The ideas are basically not new, but Kandinsky applies them differently and expands their range.

Concerning the Spiritual in Art is an exceedingly difficult book, but Kandinsky is dealing with a very difficult subject. It is not made easier by his style although this may be partly excused on the grounds that he was not writing in his mother tongue. But he seems sometimes to be wilfully obscure; his metaphysics are frequently impenetrable and his arguments unclear. Kandinsky can, in fact, be held responsible for a good deal of modern art jargon. The book is nevertheless of vital importance, not only for an understanding of Kandinsky's art but also for its effect on subsequent developments in painting. There are some passages of brilliant insight

and he at least understood the general problem that abstract, non-objective art needs definite communicable content if it is to be art and not mere decoration.

While Kandinsky had been at work on his first piece of major theory, developments were taking place in the Munich art world. After discussions between Jawlensky and his friends, a new association of artists had been formed. Jawlensky, the Russian whom Kandinsky had known at Azbé's school, had become one of the most interesting of the advanced artists in Munich. The New Artists' Association was formed to give the young artists a chance to exhibit and to present a unified front against reactionary officialdom. Kandinsky became the first chairman of the group and the first exhibition was staged in 1909. Like the earlier Munich group, *Phalanx*, the *Neue Künstlervereinigung München*, invited many foreign artists to exhibit in Germany for the first time—Braque, Picasso and Derain were shown in their exhibitions, for example. Munich was suddenly presented with an artistic situation as advanced as any in Europe.

The group, however, was not unified. The members in no sense represented a school and their achievement and talent was very uneven. Kandinsky never stopped talking about the complete lack of accomplishment and ideas of his fellow members. In his eyes, some of them actually damaged the reputation of the association. From the beginning there were two factions, one of which Kandinsky led. The relationship between them became so critical that at the beginning of 1911 Kandinsky resigned from the chairmanship. Later in the same year he, Franz Marc, Alfred Kubin and Münter left the association; Jawlensky and Marianne von Werefkin, differing somewhat from Kandinsky in their views, remained until 1912.

After the period of productive solitude in Murnau, Kandinsky once again developed a taste for art politics and with Marc decided to organise his own exhibitions. After a few months the first exhibition of the *Blaue Reiter* was held—in December 1911. The *Blaue Reiter*, or Blue Rider, is one of the most celebrated names in modern art. It is often thought that it was the title given to a distinct group of artists in Munich working in a similar direction, rather like that earlier German Expressionist group *Die Brücke*, the Bridge. This is not so. The name was first given to a publication, an almanac, specifically devoted to artists' problems, theoretical rather than practical. This almanac, an extensive document of essays, poetry and music, appeared only once, and was edited by Kandinsky and Franz Marc, whose joint idea it was. The editorial board also organised exhibitions of the work of German and foreign artists in Munich, in connection with the almanac.

It is not known who invented the name *Blaue Reiter*, or what is its real significance. Riders on horseback were, of course, one of Kandinsky's major preoccupations (the design on the cover of the almanac harks back to some of his earlier paintings). Moreover, the colour blue had strong emotional and spiritual connotations for many German Romantic poets and painters—Novalis' *Blaue Blume*, for example.

The almanac was published in the same year and by the same publisher as *Concerning the Spiritual in Art*. The articles, essays and reproductions it contained have an enormous range and show the multitude of new and vitally important subjects and topics in which the Munich artists, composers and writers were interested. The composers Schoenberg, Alban Berg and Anton von Webern contributed articles and actual musical scores. Examples of primitive art, folk art and children's drawings were reproduced, together with paintings by Cézanne, Rousseau and the Parisian avant-garde. Kandinsky also wrote an article for the almanac, *Über die Formfrage* (Concerning the Problem of Form), which in many ways is as important a statement of his beliefs as *Concerning the Spiritual in Art*. It deals with the same problems, but in a less discursive way. Its style is tighter and its logic clearer. It does not, however, contribute very much more to an understanding of Kandinsky's theories than *Concerning the Spiritual in Art*.

The exhibitions were equally important. Entirely international in their range, they showed the work of artists from Russia, Europe and America and made Munich familiar with the Constructivists, the Cubists, the Futurists and with the practitioners of almost all the other 'isms' which have become of vital importance to the history of the art in our century.

When the first World War broke out, Kandinsky decided to leave Germany and return to Russia. He went by way of Switzerland and arrived in Moscow just before Christmas 1914. Gabriele Münter did not go with him, and apart from a brief meeting in Sweden in February 1916, they never met again. In 1917 he married a second time, a Russian, Nina de Andreevskaya.

Kandinsky had never lost contact with Russia. He corresponded with various artists in his homeland, contributed articles to Russian art journals, and was well known there. When, in the early years of the Revolution, Russian art was being dramatically brought up to date and revitalised, Kandinsky became deeply involved with the organisation and administration of certain aspects of the artistic revival. He founded the Museum for Pictorial Culture, became a Professor at Moscow University, although he never taught there, and helped to edit an encyclopedia of fine arts.

Kandinsky had little time for his own work. He was not in any case stimulated by that of the other artists in Moscow, even though people like Tatlin, Malevich, Gabo and Pevsner were producing abstract work of profound originality and consequence. Some of these artists, notably the Constructivists, actually regarded Kandinsky as an opponent and he was never made to feel very welcome. After the Bolsheviks seized power, Kandinsky began to have political doubts.

Events had moved so quickly and and were of such enormity that Kandinsky felt overwhelmed. He wanted a new start.

At the age of fifty-five, in December 1921, Kandinsky and his wife returned to Germany and stayed for a time in Berlin. Times were difficult. The country was going through political and economic crises of huge proportions. Artistically the capital was different too, and the most advanced artists there, Dadaists and the followers of the *Neue Sachlichkeit* (The New Objectivity) differed radically from Kandinsky.

When, therefore, he was offered a post at the Bauhaus in 1922, Kandinsky gladly accepted. Founded by Walter Gropius in Weimar in 1919, the Bauhaus was a school of creative art, design, building and craftsmanship. As its name implies, it was in fact a workshop which attempted to unite art and craft which had for so long been regarded as separate activities. It gave a new direction to aesthetics and to the actual practice of teaching, a direction which not only revolutionised art teaching throughout Europe but is still being followed, perhaps too rigorously, in some art schools today. Because of the anti-specialist emphasis of the Bauhaus, Kandinsky was not required to teach painting, but was asked to devise a basic course in form and harmony which might benefit all manner of artists, designers and craftsmen. The curriculum of the Bauhaus was certainly to Kandinsky's liking. He had always been interested in the synthesis of the various arts and had been involved in activities along similar lines in Moscow. Moreover, as a lover of Wagner, he was constantly searching for ways in which all the arts—music, dance, theatre, painting—might be combined into one grand *Gesamtkunstwerk*, Wagner's phrase for a complete work of art. At the Bauhaus, he tried many experiments towards this end. He would, for example, paint a picture which a musician looked at and then used as inspiration for a composition. A dancer would then devise movements in keeping with the music. All this was very much the sort of thing

10   Orange. Lithograph. 1923. 16⅛ × 15 in. (41 × 38 cm.)

Walter Gropius intended. 'Our ultimate goal', he said, 'which is still far off, is the unified work of art, the "great work", in which no distinction between monumental and decorative art will remain'.

Kandinsky was a good teacher, always experimenting, always devising new ways of broadening the experience and perceptive ability of his students. He was perhaps too demanding, filling those he taught with a sense of awe, sometimes even of fear. Klee gave his students almost unlimited freedom, but Kandinsky tended to be dogmatic and prescriptive.

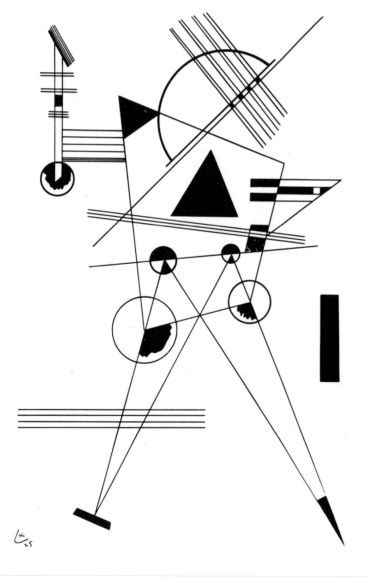

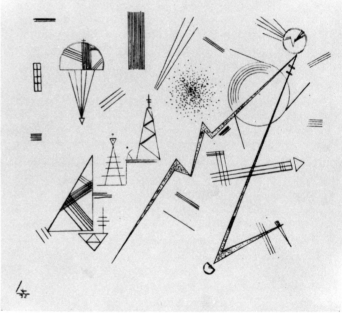

11 Lithographie: Komposition I (Lithograph: Composition I) 1925. 13×8¼ in. (33×21 cm.)

12 Radierung für den Kreis der Freunde des Bauhauses (etching for the Circle of Friends of the Bauhaus) 1932. 8×9 in. (20×24 cm.)

The Bauhaus was breaking new ground in teaching and art theory and there were no text books. Both Klee and Kandinsky wrote their own. Kandinsky's second major theoretical work, *Point and Line to Plane*, was written with his students in mind and has something of the character of a teaching manual. Published by the Bauhaus in 1926, it was concerned with the graphic elements in art and with their composition. In *Concerning the Spiritual* Kandinsky had been anxious to develop a logical system for the application of colour and now he turned naturally to the problems of form. If anything *Point and Line to Plane* is even more complex and difficult than *Concerning the Spiritual*, but it shows that Kandinsky was well read in contemporary psychology, particularly the psychology of perception, and that he applied the findings of psychologists to art.

The Weimar city fathers had opposed the Bauhaus from the beginning and they finally made it impossible for Gropius and his staff to continue to work there. The Bauhaus was moved to Dessau in 1925 and Kandinsky went with it. In 1932 it was moved again, to Berlin, where a year later it was closed down by the Nazis who feared it as a source of dangerous liberal ideas. The staff were producing the kind of modern art the Nazis most abhorred and which they later classified as 'degenerate'. Kandinsky, appreciating the implications of the situation and believing that war was imminent, decided to leave the country for Paris and a more liberal climate of thought. He hoped that things might eventually improve and that he might be able to return to Germany. He never did, for the situation was still not resolved at the time of his death in 1944.

Kandinsky learned a great deal from the Bauhaus and from his colleagues on the staff. Consideration of the paintings he produced from 1922 onwards demonstrates the magnitude of the changes which can be attributed to his experiences there. He learned most of all from Klee, whom he had known in Munich and who became his closest friend.

Compared with the upheavals of revolutionary Russia and of the moves made by the Bauhaus, Kandinsky's life in Paris was serene and uneventful. He found himself at the centre of an artistic capital without equal anywhere in the world. He met at last the great pioneers of abstract art—Miró and Mondrian, for example. He renewed his acquaintance with the Constructivist master, Pevsner, whom he had first met in Moscow with his brother, Naum Gabo.

In Paris, Kandinsky's paintings became richer. He achieved a deep and satisfying synthesis of organic and geometric forms in his compositions. His colours became more varied and more adventurous. It was as though he had come full circle, for these last paintings are essentially un-European, more oriental and even more specifically Russian. They bear the stamp of Russian folk art which Kandinsky had discovered and by which he had been profoundly influenced years before, in the province of Vologda.

It was as if, after his essentially disciplined, almost classical work at the Bauhaus, he finally discovered a way of releasing his national character on his canvas. For all his years abroad, for all his changes of nationality (he had now acquired French citizenship), he was still the Russian, believing in mysteries, in the power of the emotions.

Meanwhile his fears of Nazi policy towards the arts were further confirmed. In 1937 fifty-seven of his paintings were confiscated by the government, labelled 'degenerate' and sold in an enormous sale in Switzerland, together with the works of many other modern artists from German collections. He became convinced of the inevitability of war and wrote that the opposing nations were 'tuning their instruments as though before the performance of a great symphony'.

Apart from trips to Italy and the Pyrenees, he remained happily in Paris with his wife. When he died on 13 December 1944, he was internationally recognised as one of the major geniuses of this century. Kandinsky remains a complex personality. During his life-time he wandered over Europe and the influences which formed his art were as many as they were complicated. In some miraculous way his personality, experience, ideas, and the events and influences of his life combined in him to give birth to the revolutionary idea of abstract art. The effects of this revolution are still being felt. Kandinsky is still very much alive today—in the ideas and paintings of his disciples.

Biographical outline

1866 Kandinsky born in Moscow on December 4.

1869 Visit to Italy with his parents. Even at this age it makes a lasting impression on him.

1871 Family moves to Odessa where Kandinsky goes to the Gymnasium and has private lessons in drawing and music.

1886 Begins his studies at Moscow University where he specialises in jurisprudence and national economics.

1889 Expedition to the province of Vologda where he sees folk art for the first time. Sees Rembrandts in the Hermitage, St Petersburg. Short trip to Paris.

1893 Becomes lecturer in jurisprudence.

1895 Sees exhibition of French Impressionists in Moscow where he is profoundly affected by one of Monet's *Haystack* series.

1896 Offered Chair of Law in University of Dorpat. Refuses it and goes to Munich to study painting.

1897 Azbé School in Munich where he meets Jawlensky and Werefkin. Remains until 1899.

1900 Studies with Stuck at the Munich Academy.

1901 Founds *Phalanx* group.

1902 Becomes president of *Phalanx*, starts the *Phalanx* school where Gabriele Münter studies.

1903 *Phalanx* school closed. Various trips abroad.

1904 *Phalanx* group breaks up. Takes Münter to Italy and Tunisia where they stay until 1905.

1905 Exhibits at the Salon d'Automne, Paris. Stays at Rapallo until April 1906.

1909 Buys house at Murnau where he begins to develop new style in the Murnau landscapes. Foundation of the *Neue Künstlervereinigung* with Kandinsky as its first president. Paints first *Improvisations*.

1910 Meets Franz Marc. Writing *Concerning the Spiritual in Art* and painting first *Compositions*.

1911 Meets Paul Klee, Arp and Macke. Founds *Blaue Reiter* with Marc. First *Blaue Reiter* exhibition.

1912 Publication of *Concerning the Spiritual in Art*.

1914 After the outbreak of the war goes to Moscow by way of Switzerland.

1917 Marries Nina Andreevskaya.

1918 Various official art posts.

1919 Organises twenty-two provincial museums.

1921 Leaves Russia for Berlin.

1922 Goes to teach at the Bauhaus in Weimar.

1925 Bauhaus moves to Dessau. Kandinsky goes with it.

1926 *Point and Line to Plane* published by the Bauhaus, partly for Kandinsky's sixtieth birthday celebrations.

1928 Becomes a German citizen.

1932 Bauhaus moves to Berlin.

1933 Bauhaus closed by Nazi government. Kandinsky goes to Paris.

1934 Becomes a French citizen.

1944 Dies 13th December.

Selected book list

Kandinsky's own writings are given with the original German titles. The dates are of the first, German, editions. Where they exist English translations are also listed.

WRITINGS BY KANDINSKY

Über das Geistige in der Kunst Munich, 1912

Concerning the Spiritual in Art No 5 of Documents of Modern Art. New York, 1947

Rückblicke 1901-1913 an autobiographical sketch first published by *der Sturm*. Berlin, 1913

Rückblicke Moscow, 1918

In Memory of Wassily Kandinsky Museum of Non-Objective Painting (English translation of the second version of *Rückblicke*, Moscow 1918) New York 1945

Punkt und Linie zu Fläche Bauhausbücher 9 Munich, Langen, 1926

Point and Line to Plane: Contribution to the Analysis of the Pictorial Elements Museum of Non-Objective Painting, New York, 1947

Essays über Kunst und Künstler a selection of Kandinsky's essays. Edited by Max Bill. Second edition, Bern, 1964

BOOKS ON KANDINSKY

Kandinsky Will Grohmann. Thames and Hudson, London 1959
The definitive work on Kandinsky's life and art

ARTICLES

Kandinsky's At Rest (Rühe). Charlton Lecture on Art, L. D. Ettlinger. University of Durham. Oxford University Press 1961

Some Unpublished Letters of Kandinsky Troels Andersen. Artes, Volume II, 1966, Copenhagen

Art in the Epoch of the Great Spiritual: occult elements in the early theory of abstract painting Sixten Ringbom. The Warburg and Courtauld Journal, Volume 29, 1966. Pages 386-418

Notes on the illustrations

THE BLACK AND WHITE ILLUSTRATIONS

These are from the Gabriele Münter Foundation, Städtische Galerie, Munich.

Although Kandinsky produced woodcuts, lithographs and etchings from the beginning until the end of his artistic career, his graphic work is often overlooked, partly because it has not been easy of access. So interested was he in graphic art that for some time after the conclusion of his law studies the artist took charge of a printing shop in Moscow producing reproductions of art works. The early woodcuts probably show more of Kandinsky's direction than the related oil and tempera studies. They also show more of their Russian antecedents, a fact which emerges strongly if these early prints are compared with the work of contemporary Russian artists—Bakst, Benois, and Ssomov, for example, which show great similarities in both form and content. From the beginning Kandinsky displayed a great knowledge of the actual craftsmanship involved in the production of prints. The woodcuts, etchings and lithographs reveal a sensitive understanding of materials, not only in terms of wood and metal, but also in the precise choice of paper.

THE COLOUR PLATES

Plate 1 *The Sluice.* 1901. Oil on cardboard. 34½ × 22 in. (87 × 55 cm.). Gabriele Münter Foundation, Städtische Galerie, Munich.
In 1901, the year Kandinsky left Stuck's class at the Art Academy, he concentrated on oil studies and tempera compositions. The compositions are all imaginative and Romantic in feeling. The studies on the other hand are of various aspects of landscape and were painted directly from nature. *The Sluice*, which is very small, was painted with a palette knife in thick strokes. The general darkness of tone and the sombre atmosphere is broken here and there by small patches of bright colour which are, in their intensity, essentially anti-naturalistic. The high horizon line and the almost vertical lines of the bank tend to flatten the composition so that the painting can be 'read' as a flat pattern as well as a direct study from nature. This compositional device, in keeping with the general tendency of painting at that time, together with the hesitant use of heightened colour, show that Kandinsky was already more interested in making a painting than in reproducing an aspect of nature as realistically as possible. *The Sluice* exists in two versions and is based on a motif taken from the estate of the artist's sister-in-law.

Plate 2 *The Blue Rider.* 1903. Oil on canvas. 20½ × 21½ in. (49 × 52 cm.). Collection, Ernst Bührle, Zurich.
Horses and riders exercised a strong hold over Kandinsky's imagination. As a child his favourite toy was a painted horse, an object so powerfully evocative that he talks about it at some length in his autobiography. Kandinsky painted a number of canvases with similar subjects and it is interesting to compare this picture with the *Romantic Landscape* of 1911 (plate 16). In the *Blue Rider* the treatment is more lyrical, less dramatic. The atmosphere, like that of the fairy tales Kandinsky loved to hear from his grandmother, links the painting with the more explicitly imaginative and 'Romantic' paintings of the same period and of which the *Russian Beauty in a Landscape* of 1905 (plate 4) is a good example. The approach and technique is rather different from the work Kandinsky was doing at this time. The small, thickly applied spots in a multitude of colours remind one of some paintings by Monet. In both technique and subject it also bears a striking resemblance to the work of the Nabi painter, K. X. Roussell, whose work Kandinsky may have seen. Franz Marc, another Munich painter and a friend of Kandinsky, was painting his blue horses at about the same time. Marc joined Kandinsky seven years later to edit *The Almanac of the Blue*

Rider (see introduction) which gave its name to a series of very important exhibitions in the Bavarian capital. No one is sure exactly how the almanac got its name, but when Kandinsky and Marc were thinking about titles for it, they must at some stage have remembered this painting by Kandinsky which, because of its subject and the way in which he later developed it, ranks as a particularly important work in the artist's production.

Plate 3 *Beach Baskets in Holland*. 1904. Oil on cardboard. 9½ × 13 in. (24×33 cm.). Gabriele Münter Foundation, Städtische Galerie, Munich.

This picture was painted during a trip to Holland and its scarcely recognisable subject-matter is a group of wickerwork baskets, of the kind in which holiday-makers sit on some of the Dutch beaches. Kandinsky's palette knife technique progressed so dramatically that by 1904 he was able to control all thicknesses of paint and use them to the best advantage, not only to indicate form and weight, but also to unite the surface texture of the composition. Here areas or blotches of thick paint are contrasted with more delicate and thinner areas of pigment which add to the impression of bright sunlight and warmth. Kandinsky here uses a wide range of colours in an extremely subtle way, often applying a number of related colours in a single knife-stroke. The most interesting thing about it, however, is the degree to which the artist has broken down the surface appearance of the subject in terms of the sunlight in which it is bathed. The high horizon line not only makes the composition harder to 'read', but also places more importance on the foreground than there would be in a painting made from a more conventional viewpoint. More important than the subject itself is the play of colour and light, in which Kandinsky was far more interested. Without the example of the Impressionists, both French and German, such a picture would be inconceivable.

Plate 4 *Russian Beauty in a Landscape*. 1905. Tempera on black paper. 16¼ × 11 in. (41 × 28 cm.). Gabriele Münter Foundation, Städtische Galerie, Munich.

This picture, in tempera on a black ground, is composed of a mosaic of irregular spots of colour. It is one of the best examples of the 'Romantic' compositions which Kandinsky was painting at the same time as his near-Impressionist landscape studies. Its colour range is limited with the occasional use of a brilliant spot of, say, vermilion, and the result is a picture of great charm and decorative power. Related to *Jugendstil* both in its choice of subject-matter and in its decorative qualities, the *Russian Beauty* seems to exist in no definite place and at no definite time. In his autobiography Kandinsky describes how he tried 'like many children and young people to write poems which I eventually tore up'. These poems were written in an attempt to put down on paper and capture certain very powerful experiences, 'which demanded from me something incomprehensible which pressed on my heart during the day, filled my soul with a feeling of unease, and at night coloured my dreams with horror and joy'. He goes on to say: 'I don't remember any more whether these symbols extinguished this state of mine, i. e., that they enabled me to exist beyond space and time so that I was unable to feel myself any longer'. There is no doubt that these fantastic paintings served to fulfil a similar function, and also acted as an outlet for homesickness: 'At that time I tried, by means of lines and by distribution of mottled points of colour to express the musical spirit of Russia. Other pictures of that period reflected the contradictions and later the eccentricities of Russia'.

Plate 5 *Santa Margherita*. 1906. Oil on canvas-board. 9½ × 14¼ in. (24×38 cm.). Gabriele Münter Foundation, Städtische Galerie, Munich.

Kandinsky was fond of travel. Between 1903 and 1907 he

visited most of Germany's major cities, and also went to Italy, Russia, North Africa, France and Switzerland. From 1906 to 1907, he lived in Sèvres. It is perhaps significant that he made no extended trips to Paris during this period. It was a crucial time for the artist. He was making himself acquainted with Western Europe, and at the same time was trying to learn to stand on his own feet as an artist. In some notes he made for a lecture in 1914 he said that there were two distinct periods in his work before the breakthrough came at Murnau (see introduction). These periods were 'the dilettante period of his childhood with vague, predominantly painful stirrings, impregnated with a nostalgia incomprehensible to him' and 'the period after school, when these stirrings gradually acquired more definite form'. *Santa Margherita* was painted during Kandinsky's second trip to Italy, when he visited the Riviera. The palette knife technique clearly relates it to landscape studies such as *The Sluice* (plate 1), although here the heavy strokes of paint are applied more freely and with greater confidence. Notice how the direction of the strokes not only helps to indicate the nature of the objects depicted, but also gives the picture a coherent form—see the strokes on the surface of the water and on the reflected houses, for example. Kandinsky's colours are much brighter here than they are in pictures related to *The Sluice*. The houses, with their delicate pastel colours emerge, bathed in sunlight with the rich shadows of the hills behind. This is not a radically original painting, but at this time the artist's thinking was far ahead of his actual work. Gabriele Münter said that when she was with Kandinsky in Tunis in 1905, he told her he had already thought about producing pictures without objects.

Plate 6 *Die Nacht* (*Night*). 1907. Tempera on paper. 11½ × 19½ in. (30×49 cm.). Gabriele Münter Foundation, Städtische Galerie, Munich.

The subject of this picture is more obviously allied to the world of the fairy tale than is the *Russian Beauty* (plate 4), and reminds one of certain stories by the Brothers Grimm. There is a beautiful girl combing her hair, a child and an old hag, possibly a witch, who beckons in a menacing way. Kandinsky was well acquainted with both German and Russian fairy stories. The German ones he first heard from his grandmother, who spoke German, and they made a deep impression on him. When he saw Munich it was as though he was living in the world of the fairy tale: 'I felt as though a miraculous power, against all the laws of nature, had displaced me from century to century ever deeper into the past...'

The technique of *The Night* is similar to that of the *Russian Beauty*. The use of light spots on a dark ground recalls the woodcut, a medium which Kandinsky used a great deal from about 1910. The subjects of the woodcuts, too, are closely related to those of the 'romantic' compositions.

Plate 7 *The Elephant*. 1908. Oil on cardboard. 18×27 in. (46×68.5 cm.). Collection, Madame Nina Kandinsky, Neuilly-sur-Seine.

This charming picture, unusually exotic even for Kandinsky's imaginative compositions, brings to mind the colour and subject-matter of near eastern miniatures.

Plate 8 *Street in Murnau with Women*. 1908. Oil on canvas. 27⅝ × 37⅜ in. (70 × 94 cm.). Musée d'Art Moderne, Paris.

Although the Murnau pictures are related to the work of the Fauves which Kandinsky had seen in Paris, it would be wrong to describe them even as 'Fauvist'. The colours are highly emotional and in combinations used in such a way as to make them more intense and even more aggressive. The composition is similar to that of *Murnau with Rainbow* (plate

10) and it is instructive to compare the two. In *Street in Murnau with Women*, the form, weight and mass of the houses are pronounced, lending the subject a forbidding quality. The three figures are of great importance. Pushed to the bottom corner and cut off by the edge of the canvas they give no idea of the scale, nor do they assist the perspective (as figures obviously do in more traditional paintings). With their characterless faces they have become part of the pervading atmosphere, and the atmosphere, emotionally charged, is given a new dimension because the people are there. *Murnau with Rainbow* is more distant from us, more an object of contemplation. Here we are involved with the picture, surrounded by the atmosphere because we become involved with the figures.

Plate 9 *Murnau, Grüngasse*. 1909. Oil on cardboard. 13× 44½ in. (33 × 111 cm.). Gabriele Münter Foundation, Städtische Galerie, Munich.
In his autobiography Kandinsky says of some of his Murnau studies: '...I let myself go. I thought little of houses and trees, but applied coloured stripes and spots to the canvas with the knife and made them sing out as strongly as I could. Within me sounded the memory of early evening in Moscow, before my eyes was the strong, colour-saturated scale of the Munich light and atmosphere, which thundered deeply in the shadows'.

Plate 10 *Murnau with Rainbow*. 1909. Oil on cardboard. 13×17½ in. (33 × 44 cm.). Gabriele Münter Foundation, Städtische Galerie, Munich.
This dramatic picture gives an excellent insight into Kandinsky's intentions during the Murnau period. Its colours are either heightened or arbitrary, its perspective distorted and the pigment has been applied in a flurry of brushstrokes. By this means he dramatises the atmosphere, a break in a

storm, and also reveals something of the artist's emotions as he was painting the picture. There is little black in it, and the strongly coloured shadows emphasise the slightly unreal feeling of the scene.

Plate 11 *Painting with Houses*. 1909. Oil on canvas. 38¼× 51½ in. (97×130 cm.). Stedelijk Museum, Amsterdam.
The difference between this picture and the previous studies and compositions could hardly be more dramatic. The new start Kandinsky made at Murnau (see introduction) seems to show he was unhappy with the technique and approach of his earlier work.
At first the Murnau landscapes were painted from nature, although their colours are non-naturalistic, harsh and bright, rather in the manner of the French Fauves. Increasingly, however, Kandinsky began to paint from memory, composing freely with the raw material of houses, trees and people. Eventually the links with the original landscape became extremely slender, as here, where the perspective is as violently distorted as the colour. There is no literal division into foreground, middle ground and background, and the subject is dominated by the free expressionist play of colour and brush-stroke. The actual motif has, in fact, become the skeleton on which the artist has hung his extreme emotional reactions to it.

Plate 12 *Horses*. 1909. Oil on cardboard. 38⅛×42⅛ in. (96 × 107 cm.). Gabriele Münter Foundation, Städtische Galerie, Munich.
'The horse carries the rider with power and speed. But the rider controls the horse. Talent carries the artist to great heights with power and speed. But the artist directs his talent. That is the element of "consciousness", of "calculation" in the work—or whatever else one chooses to call it'. Kandinsky *Autobiography*

Plate 13 *Improvisation 6 (African)*. 1909. Oil on canvas. 42⅛×37¼ in. (107 ×96cm.). Gabriele Münter Foundation, Städtische Galerie, Munich.

Until he achieved a mature style Kandinsky would produce pictures in different styles concurrently. Earlier, in Munich, he had painted the landscape studies and the imaginative compositions. As he felt his way towards completely non-figurative art, the number of approaches increased and he painted landscapes concurrently with what he called 'Improvisations' and 'Compositions'. In *Concerning the Spiritual in Art* he said that the *Improvisations* were produced from a sudden and unconscious inner impulse, while the *Compositions* were more consciously controlled and often more complex pieces. This picture, one of the earliest and finest of the *Improvisations* is a recollection of Tunis which he visited in 1904. Its most interesting qualities come from the balance which exists between reality and colours and forms for their own sake. The two figures in the foreground perform a crucial role in the overall play of colour, form and rhythm.

Plate 14 *Study for Autumn 1*. 1910. Oil on cardboard. 13× 17¾ in. (34×45 cm.). Gabriele Münter Foundation, Städtische Galerie, Munich.

Here we can see how, on one level at least, Kandinsky set about evolving an abstract language. At first his pictures were abstracted from nature; in other words a landscape or scene was used to provide the raw material, the colours, lines and forms, with which the picture was primarily to exist. Here the essentials of his subject are captured in a bare way, and in the completed picture, for which this is a study, a further step has been taken away from reality. A Bavarian village lying between mountains is described by a paraphrase of a few lines and colours. The colours, which have no definite limits, capture precisely the rich mood of autumn. Although the means look simple enough they are

in fact extremely complex: each line has a different character from the next and each describes a type of building or the side of a mountain with extreme economy but great precision. In this way Kandinsky acquired a vocabulary of forms and colours which he later used in completely abstract pictures and it is interesting to trace their development in a succession of canvases.

Plate 15 *First Abstract Watercolour*. 1910. Watercolour. 19¾× 25½ in. (50×65 cm.). Collection, Madame Nina Kandinsky, Neuilly-sur-Seine.

This is Kandinsky's first completely non-figurative painting. He produced it in the year in which he was writing his theoretical justification for abstract art, *Concerning the Spiritual in Art*. Although he was thinking about the new art as early as this (in fact even earlier), actual paintings produced in the same spirit are extremely rare and all are watercolours. The final leap to abstract painting took much longer and he was still painting recognisable objects as late as 1913 alongside more abstract work. However, there are several watercolours which show that he was prepared to experiment in the less permanent medium much earlier. This picture, therefore, has closer links with Kandinsky's later work and is very different from anything else done at the same time. The artist was clearly pleased with the result. He rarely signed his watercolours, but he signed this one.

Plate 16 *Romantic Landscape*. 1911. Oil on canvas. 37×51⅛ in. (94×129 cm.). Gabriele Münter Foundation, Städtische Galerie, Munich.

This is one of Kandinsky's most exciting and successful early paintings. The subject and title hark back to his previous Munich period where his fascination for horses and riders was first revealed. One of his most memorable childhood experiences was being given a toy horse and there is no doubt that the name *Blue Rider* came from Kandinsky. Here the mood, the speed and energy of the riders, the landscape accelerating past are all described in the barest possible way. The composition, brush strokes varying from the broad stroke to the dot all show a supreme confidence which is barely perceptible in any of his earlier work.

Plate 17 *All Saints Picture 11*. 1911. Oil on cardboard. 22½ × 26 in. (57 × 66 cm.). Gabriele Münter Foundation, Städtische Galerie, Munich.

'In many ways art is similar to religion. Its development consists not in new discoveries which invalidate the old truths (as is obviously the case in science). Its development consists in sudden illuminations, similar to lightning, in explosions, which burst in the sky like fireworks... this illumination shows with blinding light new perspectives, new truths, which are basically nothing but the organic development, the further organic growth of the earlier wisdom... was the New Testament possible without the Old? Could our time, that of the threshold of the "third" revelation, be thinkable without the second?' Kandinsky *Autobiography*

Plate 18 *Saint George 1*. 1911. Oil on canvas. 37¾ × 41½ in. (95 × 105 cm.). Collection, Professor W. Löffler, Zurich.

The years before Kandinsky turned exclusively to abstract painting are marked by a great variety of styles and subjects. The artist was a profoundly religious man and attached both intellectually and emotionally to the Russian Orthodox Church which he visited whenever he could. He turned to religious subjects, perhaps partly in an attempt to find the raw material through which he might express the hidden truths which he wanted to make the content of his art. He not only painted St George four times (three canvases and one glass painting), but also the Resurrection of the Dead, the Last Judgement and the Feast of All Saints, again in

various versions and media. St George plays an important role in the liturgy of the Eastern churches and he also brings Kandinsky back once again to the motif of the horse and rider. Grohmann suggests that the whiteness and marked luminosity of this picture is intended to express the spirituality of the subject and also to emphasise the supernatural feat of the Saint. Although the painting reproduced is not the version on glass, something needs to be said about Kandinsky's use of this unusual technique. While in Murnau he discovered the paintings which some of the Bavarian peasant artists had made on glass. They had been painted in bright colours and gained enormously in richness and luminosity because of the light shining through the glass and the gloss on the surface—they were painted on the reverse side. Without exception these paintings are of religious subjects and apart from this, their very richness must have appealed to the artist who was in any case interested in folk art. He therefore did some himself—as indeed did Münter—imitating the unsophisticated technique of the originals.

Plate 19 *Woman in Moscow*. 1912. Watercolour. 42⅞ × 42⅞ in. (108 × 108 cm.). Gabriele Münter Foundation, Städtische Galerie, Munich.

There are two versions of this Russian subject, one a painting on glass, the other on canvas. It is included here because it is unique among Kandinsky's works. In its dream-like naivety and distortions, it comes close to Chagall. Grohmann suggests that the hovering shape at the top right and the disposition of colour owes something to the beliefs of theosophy in which Kandinsky was interested and which not only influenced his attitude to art in general but, more specifically, helped him to formulate his theory of abstract art.

Plate 20 *The Flood*. 1912. Oil on canvas. 39⅜ × 41⅜ in. (100 × 105 cm.). Kaiser-Wilhelm Museum, Krefeld.

This apocalyptic subject was particularly appropriate for Kandinsky's ambitious religious compositions.

Plate 21 *Improvisation 30*. 1913. Oil on canvas. 43⅝ × 43⅝ in. (110 × 110 cm.). The Art Institute of Chicago, Arthur Jerome Eddy Memorial Collection.

By 1913 Kandinsky had mastered the abstract style of expression and had evolved a versatile language of forms, lines and colours, so that he could communicate almost any experience he wished. Superficially, this *Improvisation* seems to have more connection with reality than any other of the same period. Buildings, people, mountains, cannon and cannon-blasts can be deciphered. In fact, Kandinsky adopted the sub-title 'Cannon' for his private use, but claimed that it had nothing to do with the content of the painting. The real content, he claimed, is what the viewer feels under the impact of the colour and forms. All allusions to real objects are purely accidental. Such is the power of allusion, however, that the cannon nevertheless emerges as the dominant motif of the composition. In view of the date of the painting, it has been suggested that this picture in some way heralds the approaching war. This is most improbable.

Plate 22 *Improvisation 'Klamm' (Ravine)*. 1914. Oil on canvas. 43¾ × 43¾ in. (109 × 109 cm.). Gabriele Münter Foundation, Städtische Galerie, Munich.

Kandinsky often gave his improvisations subtitles for his own private use, as quick reminders. Here the subtitle is 'Klamm' meaning 'Ravine'. It was painted after he had visited the canyon of Höllental. The free forms are mixed with naturalistic ones, a waterfall, a landing-stage and a couple in Bavarian costume.

'Painting is a thundering conflict of different worlds, which in and out of the battle with one another are intended to create the new world, which is called the work of art. Each work arises technically in a way similar to that in which the cosmos arose—through catastrophes, which from the chaotic roaring of the instruments finally create a symphony, the music of the spheres. The creation of the work is the creation of worlds'. Kandinsky *Autobiography*.

Plate 23 *Picture with Three Spots*. 1914. Oil on canvas. 46½ × 42½ in. (118 × 108 cm.). Solomon R. Guggenheim Museum, New York.

In 1914 Kandinsky produced little work, because he was interrupted by the war. He did not resume painting until 1916. Some writers have described Kandinsky's early abstract paintings in terms of a creation parallel to that of the natural world (see quotation in note to plate 22).

Form becomes coherent out of chaos. The picture, having no visual references outside itself, is therefore a microcosm, obeying its own laws and emerging in coherent form in its own way; moreover this growth, because it is determined by a man who is himself part of nature, will ultimately be governed by the same natural laws. As Kandinsky recognised, the painter's activity is here close to that of the composer, because painting has, like music, become absolute: 'Just as sounds and rhythms combine in music, so must forms and colour be unified in painting by the play of their manifold relationships'. *Picture with Three Spots* shows Kandinsky's interest in combining broad painting in large areas with graphic elements which appear to float on the surface, almost above the void. The atmosphere is dramatic, the sense of space awesome, implying chaos from which the picture emerges to take coherent form.

Plate 24 *Painting on a Light Ground*. 1916. Oil on canvas. 39½ × 30¾ in. (100 × 78 cm.). Collection, Madame Nina Kandinsky, Neuilly-sur-Seine.

In spite of Kandinsky's deep involvement with the art politics of Russia, there is much evidence to suggest that the climate did not suit him at all. In 1915 he painted nothing. This may have been simply that he was taking time to settle in and become accustomed to the fact of war, but it is significant that in the following year half his output was done during a short trip to Sweden. There are in all eight canvases from 1916 and five of these are still relatively inaccessible in Russia. *Painting on a Light Ground* is one of the Swedish pictures and is not radically different from his last Munich pictures. Although he had already come into close contact with the Russian versions of abstract art, they no longer had any effect on him.

Plate 25 *In the Black Circle*. 1923. Oil on canvas. 51⅛ × 51⅛ in. (129 × 129 cm.). Galerie Maeght, Paris.

In 1923 and 1924 Kandinsky painted many pictures either of, or based on circles. These anticipate the canvases of 1926 of which the artist was especially proud. The circle itself held a mystical significance for him; he believed that it formed a link with the cosmic. He spoke of his 'strong feeling for the inner force of the circle and its countless variations: I love the circle today as I formerly loved the horse, for instance—perhaps even more, since I find more inner potentialities in the circle which is why it has taken the horse's place...'

This picture is particularly interesting, because it shows Kandinsky's attempts at this time to achieve a synthesis between organic and geometric shapes. Here the definite outline of the circle, contained as it is within the square of the frame, makes coherent a mass of disparate elements.

Plate 26 *Silent*. 1924. Oil on cardboard. 27⅛ × 19½ in. (68 × 49 cm.). Boymans Museum, Rotterdam.

During the Bauhaus period Kandinsky greatly enlarged his vocabulary of forms and became infinitely more inventive in his use of them. This picture is a rich synthesis of disparate elements: the broad painting on the field and the variety of shapes, colours and graphic elements above it. A distinct rhythm is set up as we progress from triangle to triangle, perceiving how each is similar yet dissimilar one from the other. We go through the painting from the general to the particular until we grasp the whole. It is a finely balanced, complex composition in which contrasting movements become the basis for a delicate structure.

Plate 27 *Small Dream in Red*. 1925. Oil on canvas. 13¾ × 16⅛ in. (34 × 41 cm.). Collection, Madame Nina Kandinsky, Neuilly-sur-Seine.

This was painted before Kandinsky moved with the Bauhaus to Dessau and it is extremely interesting because it is reminiscent of paintings from the Munich period. The atmosphere is lyrical and the sense of space, created by the amorphous areas of paint on the field, recall his earlier work. So also do the graphic elements which play freely across the surface of the canvas and the mountainous shapes to the right. It is difficult not to see a boat with a funnel in this picture, but according to Kandinsky, such games of recognition have nothing to do with his intentions. The boat does not, however, conflict with the general atmosphere of the painting. This picture was the only one to be reproduced in colour in *Point and Line to Plane* so it must have had great significance for the artist.

Plate 28 *Several Circles*. 1926. Oil on canvas. 55⅛ × 55⅛ in. (140 × 140 cm.). Solomon R. Guggenheim Museum, New York.

Kandinsky was especially proud of the work he produced in 1926. In a letter to Will Grohmann, looking back on the period, he wrote: 'You mention the circle and I agree with your definition... why does the circle fascinate me? It is (1) the most modest form, but asserts itself unconditionally, (2) a precise but inexhaustible variable, (3) simultaneously stable and unstable, (4) simultaneously loud and soft, (5) a single tension that carries countless tensions within it. The circle is the synthesis of the greatest oppositions. It combines the concentric and the excentric in a single form, and in balance. Of the three primary forms (triangle, square, circle), it points most clearly to the fourth dimension'.

Plate 29 *Softened Construction*. 1927. Oil on canvas. 39½ × 19½ in. (100 × 50 cm.). Collection, Mr and Mrs Nathan Cummings, Chicago.
'Content is nothing but the sum of organised tensions. From this point of view one can discover the basic identity of the rules of composition in all arts—always accepting that the arts can only represent their object materially by means of organised reactions... already today one can safely assume that the roots of laws of compositions are the same for art as they are for nature.' Kandinsky *Analysis of the Primary Elements of Painting* 1928

Plate 30 *At Rest*. 1928. Oil on canvas. 20½ × 31⅛ in. (52 × 79 cm.). Collection, Mr and Mrs Nathan Cummings, Chicago.
No picture from the Weimar Bauhaus period better shows the effects Kandinsky sought to achieve and how he set about capturing them on canvas. The German title, *Rühe*, expresses a much more general peace and serenity than its English equivalent, and it is this sense of mood, an emotional state, that Kandinsky attempts to evoke here. His language consists of lines, forms and colours. Horizontals—lines of force which are essentially inactive—predominate, broken only by perfectly balanced verticals and curves. The arrangement, poised as it is, suggests serenity and this is emphasised

by the colours which are predominantly blue and from the lower tonal ranges. This picture may be reminiscent of a harbour with sailing boats, and it may be that Kandinsky derived the idea for his forms from a painting based on that subject, which Klee had painted at the Bauhaus shortly before this.

Plate 31 *Fixed Points*. 1929. Oil on cardboard. 27½ × 13⅝ in. (69 × 34 cm.). Collection, Mrs J. L. Wolgin, Philadelphia.

Plate 32 *Scarcely (Kaum)*. 1930. Tempera and plaster. 13¾ × 6¼ in. (34 × 15 cm.). Boymans Museum, Rotterdam.
In *Point and Line to Plane* Kandinsky devotes some space to a discussion of surfaces. They can be of various textures, he says, rough, smooth, glossy. This surface texture then becomes an important element in the composition of the picture. It can add energy to pictorial devices by contrasting with them or emphasising them, and can help to create an illusion of space or flatness. In this painting, in an unusual medium, the surface texture plays an enormous role in the creation of space and atmosphere. Kandinsky produced a great deal of work while he was at Dessau. During this time zig-zag lines and angular constructions appear repeatedly.

Plate 33 *Layers*. 1932. Tempera on cardboard. 19½ × 13¾ in. (49 × 34 cm.). Collection, Mr and Mrs Nathan Cummings, Chicago.
The Bauhaus moved from Dessau to Berlin in 1932. Some writers have seen in the work of this period a restraint and a striving for moods which approach the sombre. Restrained they certainly are, but it is a restraint resulting from a greater sureness of touch and a greater degree of confidence in what he was doing rather than a restraint in mood. There is nothing sombre about this picture. It has a richness and

beauty all the more remarkable because it has been achieved with such limited colours and means.

Plate 34 *Relations.* 1934. Oil and sand on canvas. 35×45⅝ in. (88×115 cm.). Collection, Princess E. Zalstem-Zalessky, New York.

In 1934 Kandinsky mixed sand with his oil paint for the first time, and used the technique more and more in his Paris period. He used sand to distinguish individual forms more effectively from the colour planes and to enliven the surface texture of the canvas. Here sand is used in just this way, so that the forms are given body and materiality. The colours and the forms themselves, rich and exotic, are typical of the work Kandinsky was doing at this time. They are very different from the geometric constructions of the Bauhaus and have a zoomorphic, organic appearance reminiscent of tiny organisms seen under a microscope.

Plate 35 *Black Forms on White.* 1934. Oil on canvas. 27⅝×27⅝ in. (70×70 cm.). Collection, Madame Yvonne Zervos, Paris.

The first picture Kandinsky painted after his arrival in Paris in 1933 was called, significantly enough, *Start,* and there is indeed something of a new start discernible in the work of this period. After the years at the Bauhaus, in which he was concerned predominantly with the use of geometric and regular forms, he now greatly increased his artistic vocabulary and relied more and more on non-geometric 'organic' forms for his pictures. 'Organic' forms are those which are close to the basic forms in nature without actually representing anything specific. The forms which fill this canvas are irregular, rather like amœbae. In some ways they resemble forms which Arp was using at the same time. Kandinsky's friendship with this German-French painter and sculptor dates from this period. In another sense they form

a direct link with the *Improvisations* of 1913 which, although much freer and less intellectual in their conception, also rely on an organic approach through nature to the problems of abstract composition.

This picture anticipates one of the major post-war streams of painting, particularly strong in England and America, the so-called 'hard-edge' school. These paintings rely for their effects on the interplay between figures and background, between major and minor shapes which appear now to be dominant, now to be passive.

Plate 36 *Brown with Supplement.* 1935. 31⅞ × 39⅜ in. (81×100 cm.). Boymans Museum, Rotterdam.

Kandinsky's Parisian paintings are different in colour as well as in form from those which preceded them. In place of a coolness, achieved by using a limited range of colour similar in tone, there is a sumptuousness which is almost oriental. The colours are brighter, more varied and of a greater intensity, and the texture is richer. About this time Kandinsky began to mix fine sand with his paint to differentiate the colour planes from the individual forms which float upon them.

Plate 37 *Succession.* 1935. Oil on canvas. 31⅞×39⅜ in. (81×100 cm.). Phillips Collection, Washington, D.C.

Here is yet another example of Kandinsky's constant search for a variety of forms, both organic and geometric, which can be made to cohere within the bounds of a firm order.

Plate 38 *Dominant Curve.* 1936. Oil on canvas. 50⅞×76½ in. (129×194 cm.). Solomon R. Guggenheim Museum, New York.

Plate 39 *Green Figure.* 1936. Oil on canvas. 45⅝×35 in. (115×88 cm.). Galerie Maeght, Paris.

During the last years of his life in Paris, Kandinsky returned to a more organic conception of composition. The forms he uses are less geometric, and take on the character of living organisms. This remarkable work consists of organic forms. They appear to have grown according to natural laws. The painting is remarkable for the way in which it gives an impression of richness and intricacy by means of only two colours which are flat and without modelling. There is no drawing, contours are described by the areas they touch. It is a startlingly modern picture. There is a distinct play between the figure and the field, and a spatial ambiguity created by the rough edges of the dark green area.

Plate 40 *Tensions Relaxed.* 1937. Oil on canvas. 35⅛ × 45⅞ in. (89 × 115 cm.). Collection, Willard Gidwitz, Chicago.

'Each spiritual age expresses its special character in a form which corresponds exactly to its character. Each age in this way characterises its true "physiognomy", full of expression and strength. Thus in all spiritual areas "yesterday" is transformed into "today". But apart from this, art possesses a further quality which it alone possesses: that quality which enables one to divine the "tomorrow" today—a strength which is both creative and prophetic.' *Kandinsky's last theoretical statement* 1942

Plate 41 *Sweet Trifles.* 1937. Water colour and oil on canvas. 24⅝ × 9⅞ in. (62 × 25 cm.). Collection, Madame Nina Kandinsky, Neuilly-sur-Seine.

This is perhaps the most carefully organised picture ever made by Kandinsky. It could almost be described as paintings within one painting, because each division contains something complete in itself. Each detail varies in complexity and consequently the organisation into a whole seems all the more astounding.

Plate 42 *Composition X.* 1939. Oil on canvas. 51⅛ × 76¾ in. (129 × 194 cm.). Collection, Madame Nina Kandinsky, Neuilly-sur-Seine.

It has often been said that the works of Kandinsky's Paris period are decidedly non-European in their appearance. They are almost oriental in richness of colour and complexity of design. They recall something of Russian and near eastern folk art. Kandinsky's first encounter with Russian folk art was a profound experience. It gave him, he said, the impression of walking around inside a picture (see introduction). He continued by saying that he wanted to paint pictures in which the viewer could also wander freely. Folk art, however, is decoration and Kandinsky feared that abstract art might all too easily become mere decoration. This he determined to avoid at all costs in his own painting. The subtle splendour, the intricate interplay of planes, shapes and colours in this picture may not stimulate associations, but it does inspire a mood. It is, in itself, an experience.

Plate 43 *Various Actions.* 1941. Oil and lacquer on canvas. 35 × 45⅝ in. (88 × 115 cm.). Solomon R. Guggenheim Museum, New York.

Kandinsky met Miró in 1939 and there is something of the Spaniard's influence here, in the fantastic shapes and hieroglyphic lines floating in a space which is both infinite and limited.

Plate 44 *Division-Unity.* 1943. Tempera and oil on cardboard. 22⅞ × 16½ in. (58 × 41 cm.). Collection, Madame Nina Kandinsky, Neuilly-sur-Seine.

As the war progressed, Kandinsky found it more and more difficult to obtain materials. His supplies were dwindling, so he painted more often on cardboard and limited the size of his paintings. This one, for example, in spite of its complexity, is quite small. He also prepared his own paints.

The work of these years is characterised by the combination of organic, in this case almost zoomorphic, shapes with precisely divided areas, so that each canvas is a series of actions, each series both self-contained and related to the others.

Plate 45 *Circle and Square.* 1943. Tempera and oil on cardboard. 16½ × 22⅞ in. (41 × 58 cm.). Collection, Madame Nina Kandinsky, Neuilly-sur-Seine.
The circle and square of the title are not immediately obvious, but when recognised they dominate the picture, become the focal point of the composition, and give the organic shapes, which contain circles and rectilinear configurations, meaning. The circle, square and triangle, had been a concern of Kandinsky since his days at Bauhaus. They are the three basic geometric shapes and they had, for the artist, a mystical significance. At the Bauhaus he tried a number of experiments with these three devices to see if each had a natural colour which should accompany it. He even sent questionnaires to all the students, asking each one to fill in the outline of a square, circle and triangle with the colour he considered most appropriate.

Plate 46 *Seven.* 1943. Oil on cardboard. 22⅞ × 16½ in. (58 × 41 cm.). Collection, Max Bill, Zurich.
This picture belongs to the Swiss painter and sculptor Max Bill, who studied at the Bauhaus and knew Kandinsky well. Max Bill edited the collection of essays by Kandinsky *Concerning Art and Artists.*

Plate 47 *A Conglomerate.* 1943. Gouache and oil on cardboard. 22⅞ × 16½ in. (58 × 41 cm.). Collection, Madame Nina Kandinsky, Neuilly-sur-Seine.
A striking feature of this composition is the succession of ways in which the edges of the actual painting are made to play against the various features within it. Notice first of all the yellow rectangle which is in proportion with the picture. The cut-in step at the top and the protruding elements around the edges create a tension with the edge of the picture. A similar effect is achieved by the freer curvilinear area of blue which seems to flow in from beyond the picture and surround the central motif.

Plate 48 *White Balancing Act.* 1944. Gouache and oil on cardboard. 22⅞ × 16½ in. (58 × 41 cm.). Collection, Professor W. Löffler, Zurich.

2

3

6

8

9

10

11

13

14

16

17

18

19

20

21

22

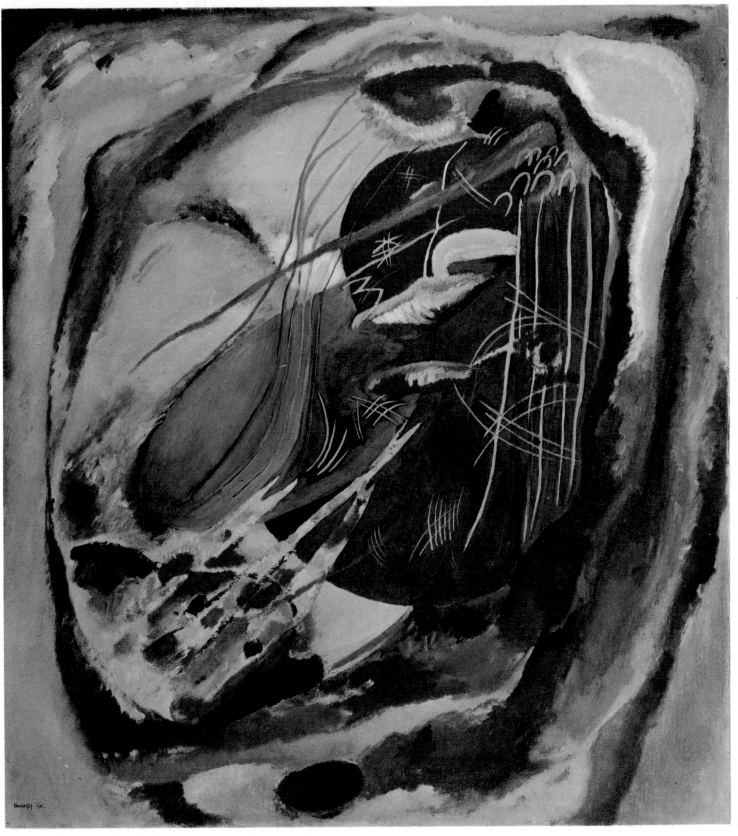

23

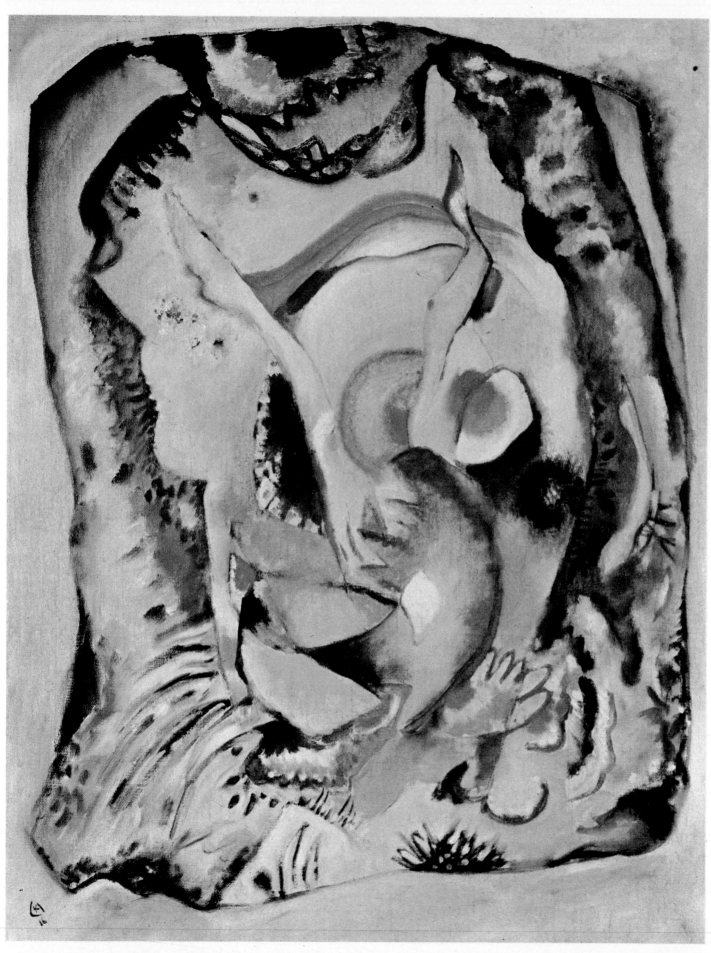

24

25

27

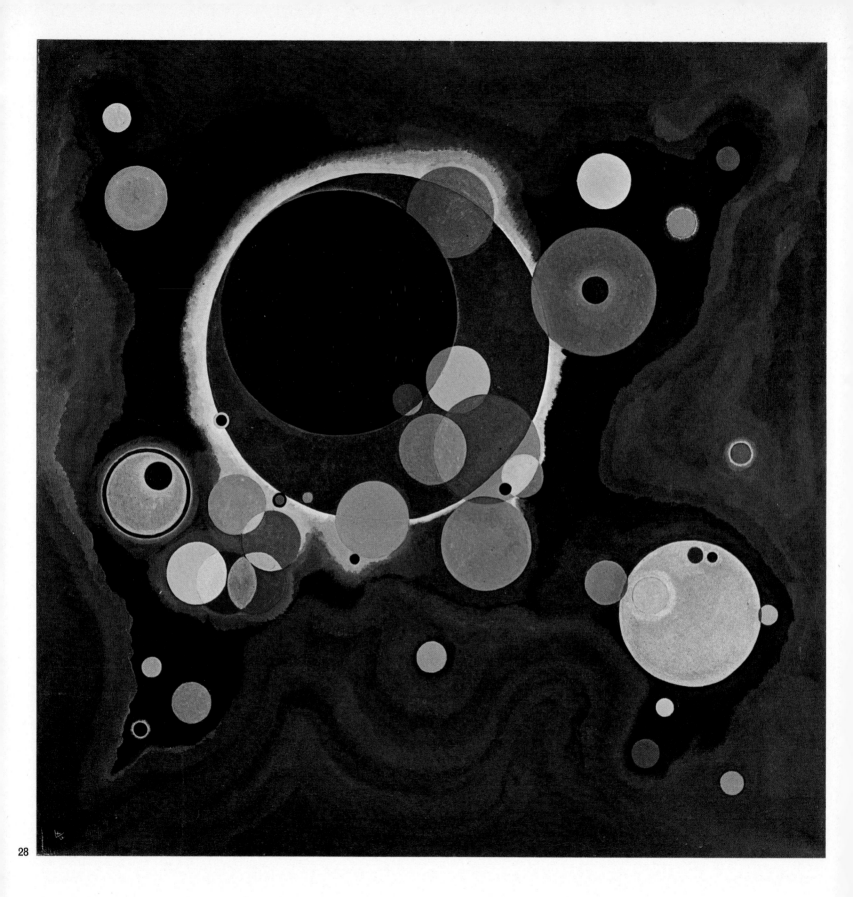

28

30

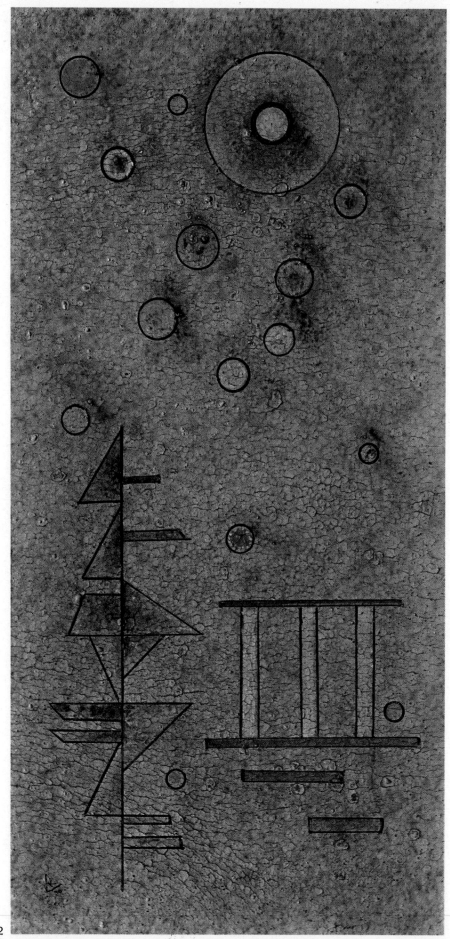

34

36

37

38

40

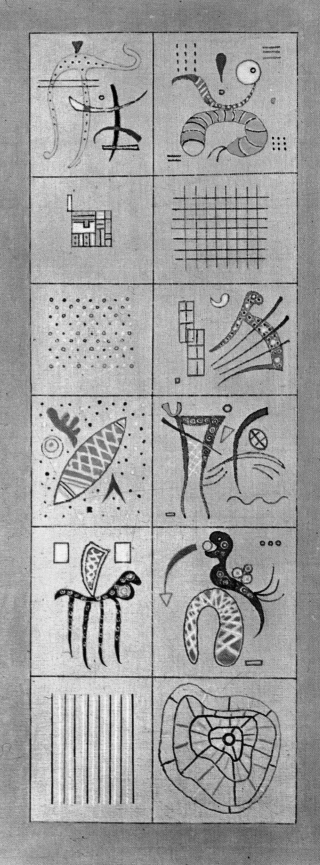

43

45

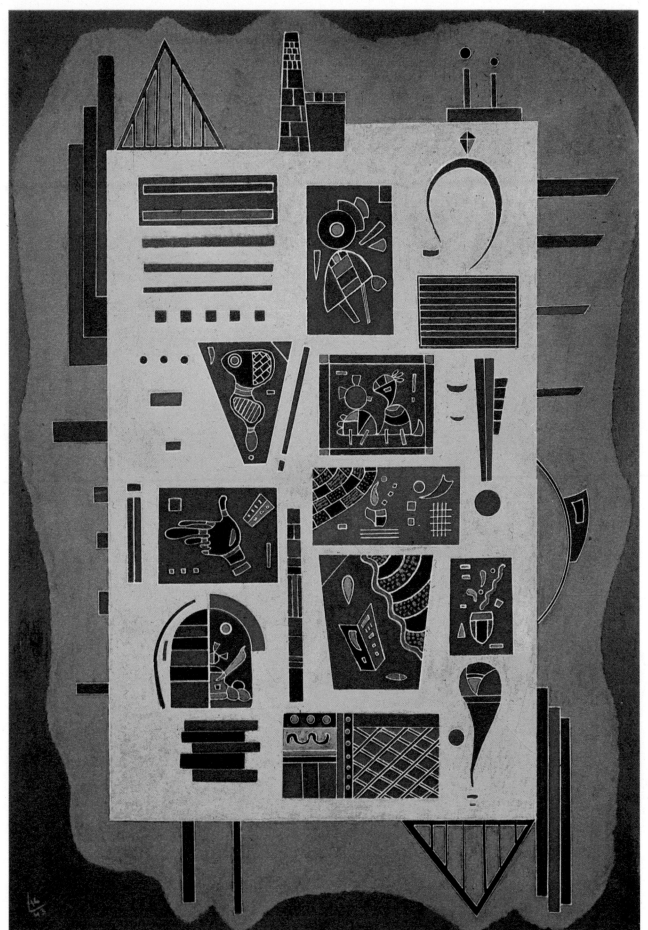

48